# PC MAKES US CRAZY

\

by Karen Kellock Ph.D.

---

## Manual for
## Superior Men

**A complete theory based on Einstein physics,
Political Psychology, Systems Theory
and Archetypal Psychiatry.**

### FORMULA

**All success attraction
All disease obstruction
All recovery elimination**

**You must fast on all three**

**OBSTRUCTIONS:**

**People
Habit
Food**

# P.C. MAKES US CRAZY

## *Shame Internalized From Abandonment*

People love to be malicious in a group:  they compete who is crueler when spreading the scoop.  They didn't know anything about her, just assumed she was nuts from what the others  inferred.  They loved being the in-group who did the judging when they had her over a barrel and struggling.   Abandonment from the pack brings shame in wolves who die of starvation: a similar situation.    The self ceases to exist psychotically, feeling unlovable, unworthy and defective. Self-compassion incinerates the nastiness dumped by relatives, healing the shame internalized with abandonment.

# FRIENDS WITH BENEFITS

A FRIEND WITH BENEFITS DROPS BY
DUMB LADIES
MISTREATMENT MAKES US COMPLY
HE'S NOT PROTECTING YOU
NO PILLOW TALK HERE
SHE'S CHEAP AND FREE
SEX IS ALL HE WANTS
YOU'RE A BAD WOMAN TO STAY
WHEN CHOSEN ONES LEAVE
THE DOWN LOW
THIS IS *NOT* A RELATIONSHIP
TREASONOUS COLLEGE KIDS
THEY WANT A BROKEN BORDER
BIDEN'S SPOILED BRATS
SAY "NO!" TO PAST THOUGHTS
DETOXING FROM MARIUJUANA
POT DETOX SUX

# FRIENDS WITH BENEFITS

*The right man will approach you in the right way: His job is to protect and provide for you lady.*

If you get involved with the wrong people don't complain when they bring hell in on you.

Cut toxic ties and shoot up like a rocket. That's our slogan for a great life without maggots.

"Friends with benefits" is all for him. He's not providing or protecting & he never takes you out friend.

## A FRIEND WITH BENEFITS DROPS BY

A friend with benefits drops by your house, you eat or watch TV then he wants sex: ridiculous!

He's just using you for sex. It's gonna be your heartbreak. Get your things and that's IT.

If he wants you he has to come correct. He has to commit to a relationship or forget it.

Friends with benefits go Dutch. That's a sure sign you're in a degrading relationship for you as such.

You pay your way/he pays his way and you have sex together. He wins out & you're in a bummer.

## DUMB LADIES

Many women do this thinking they're in a relationship and it's nothing [and costs him nothing].

It costs a man nothing to be with you--not even his time since he's out the door soon after, aye.

# FRIENDS WITH BENEFITS

No time loss to him--he comes over after dark or when he gets a minute. Women: wake up and reject!

You are NOT in a relationship so wake up/stop thinking that. Has he spent a nickel? Not that brat.

Some women let em come over at midnight for a quickie and they still think they're in a relationship see.

Ladies, we've forgotten what it feels like to be treated like queens. We allow men to dictate see.

## MISTREATMENT MAKES US COMPLY

Men have told us how to comply when mistreated, if we wanna stay with them, can you believe it?

These men believe they are the prize and we should chase after them with glee in our eyes.

They want sex free. You're not even a prostitute you're a quick stop for free and fast food sweetie.

If they can get sex like that then for sure they'll be coming around but NEVER taking you out.

A friend with benefits will NOT provide for you. That's his job if he's with you and that's a rule.

If he's not introducing you to his friends/family as his girlfriend you have nothing so wake up friend.

## HE'S NOT PROTECTING YOU

He's not protecting you. He repeats evil gossip against you and laughs: it's a horrible situation Sue.

Women: Is the sex part such a big benefit for you that you're willing to be degraded like this?

# FRIENDS WITH BENEFITS

Don't allow men to come in and just "do you" anyway they want to cuz you're lonely and blue.

Focus on your awakening & celibacy and the drive for inferior relationships will dissolve quickly.

You wanted a mate, it's a strong urge. But then his treatment made the urge worse for sure.

That urge is so strong you can't think logically or make good decisions. It's a total disaster friend.

Celibacy will wipe the slate clean so you can return to baseline and think logically again see.

## NO PILLOW TALK HERE

There's no pillow talk ever, he's gotta get back to work to make money for some other woman dear.

You're just another friend to him. He comes for sex then goes to another friend to drink/dine/watch flix.

If he wants you he will AGREE to your celibacy until the time is right--when and IF respect alights.

A man who respects you sweet Sue will take the time, money and energy it takes to BE WITH YOU.

Sweet Sue, you are a valuable person and it COSTS to be with you. Remember that or be blue.

If you have this mindset, most men in your life will be kicked out. You're a queen and very devout.

The right man will approach you in the right way: His job is to protect and provide for you lady.

## SHE'S CHEAP AND FREE

# FRIENDS WITH BENEFITS

Men will continue to do these things as long as women remain CHEAP & FREE. Come back to reality.

Women give themselves away & cry about it later when he leaves so quickly. Feel this sweetie.

When the clown comes back around you'll be ready this time with gumption and dignity, newfound.

Immature, entitled and sexually motivated. So much so he easily lies without guilt or shame for it.

## SEX IS ALL HE WANTS

If he's sexually motivated that's is ALL HE WANTS. It's not flattery, he's turned you into a slut.

If he's that way all he's looking for is someone to have sex with just like any animal in the brush.

If he shit-shots for response--talking about sex--then get away fast because he is the worst.

She may say "let's see if we're compatible in other ways" and he's not listening cuz it's all he wants ok.

Just because a man is persistent doesn't mean he's interested in you. He just wants sex Sue.

Long after he showed who he was you still loved talking to him: this encouragement was your sin.

## YOU'RE A BAD WOMAN TO STAY

After he showed an interest in sex and you stayed on it was sexy to him cuz you're a bad woman.

Try getting to know him: he's not interested in intimacy. This is an irritant cuz he just wants sex see.

# FRIENDS WITH BENEFITS

Give him a book on how to treat a queen and he'll say he's gotta get going cuz it's irrelevant see.

A book on intimacy? Well, he'll try but he's really beginning to think he's not your type.

Once you recognize his game, why would you ever keep talking to this guy the same?

## WHEN CHOSEN ONES LEAVE

As a chosen one you'll be taken for granted until it's too late. When you're gone lives go dark ok.

"Actions never lie and words don't mean shit." This is what you watch for, a most important tip.

What is a girlfriend? Well she's like a wife [cleans, cooks, sex] but without the commitment.

## THE DOWN LOW

You girls complaining about men and here it's you creating it. I did it too, it's hard forgetting it.

A bisexual is a homosexual man who will at times get in bed with a woman for whatever reason.

Any man who can be with a man sexually is a homosexual so don't call him "bisexual".

Ladies: You are not obligated to have sex just cuz he bought you dinner [that's prostitution dear].

You can be best in the world and be taken for granted but God'll pour hot coals on their head.

Bad memories are an attack: What else does Satan have to hold us back but the bad past?

# FRIENDS WITH BENEFITS

Gotta shut down anti-Israel protests or they feel entitled and bring even more disgust.

For you liberal Mormons: Sodom and Gomorrah is a latter day disease, recognize that please.

If people can't control their evil children then we gotta be like God: we're sweet, until we're NOT.

Ladies: You no longer have to bed a man just cuz he bought you dinner! Repent now dear!

Imagine this: for the price of dinner he expects sex. Think purity ladies, this is utterly ridiculous!

If you're easy he'll see you as a whore and spread gossip about you even more but purity is adored.

He has no right in the world to expect anything from you for dinner but "thank you", then it's over.

## THIS IS *NOT* A RELATIONSHIP

Stop calling everyone your "friend". It is social fascism that makes us wanna feel popular, amen.

A desire to fit in makes you miserable. Why shouldn't they fit you instead? Think this way bro'.

The minute you cut off the duds who hold you back you shoot up to success, that's a fact.

You're unequally yoked, like a horse to a donkey. You won't get anywhere this way, predictably.

Dealing with duds will only bring frustration. You don't need this, for success you need joy/elation.

## TREASONOUS COLLEGE KIDS

# FRIENDS WITH BENEFITS

Why go along with the crazy college kids dumb to what they're talking about? You're adults!

These crazy kids know nothing about the holocaust, WWII or anything else. Disgusting nuts!

Entitled brats who feel justified in ruining college for everyone else are not just an inconvenience.

They want this demented old fool Biden in again because, again, they don't know anything.

They're all for gays but unaware that in Gaza they'd be beheaded, hung or thrown off of buildings.

Their idea of democracy is one party rule and the wolf of authoritarianism in sheep's clothing.

## THEY WANT A BROKEN BORDER

They want to have a broken border for new voters. Their idea of democracy is only perpetual power.

Saving democracy means saving a doddering old fool's presidency so he can put us all in poverty.

Ignorance, conformity and evil--yes, evil--is the basis of college protests and that's the truth people.

In front of parents Hamas killed babies but college kids love em and think they're great see.

Spoiled rotten rioters had their fun today with a pizza party by the way but karma's comin' ok.

Obnoxious brats hide their faces so they can get a good job later despite what happened 7 October.

Feckless administrators are terrified to offend the silver spoon brats, can you imagine that?

# FRIENDS WITH BENEFITS

Professional protestors stir the pot. They've been thru all of em and Just like to do it, that's all.

Protesting is a beloved activity like playing golf or tennis. These libs just love to be a menace.

## BIDEN'S SPOILED BRATS

Let's just call em "Biden's Spoiled Brats" and we've hit the nail on the head, or arrest him instead.

Campus chaos is a natural outcome of brainwashing since the sixties and we all know that see.

Campus chaos has become barbarism not civilization. It's based on false tolerance not education.

The coddled kids crumbled because parents said "I love you" rather than drawing strict lines too.

They're about smashing windows and violent chants. What a great school the elite Columbia is.

The bigoted pro-terrorist rioters don't care what happened Oct. 7, in Israel's worst massacre.

White supremacy is one of the rarest crimes but when it happens we never hear the end of it, aye.

Whites all over world praying to black people: a George Soros agenda with a black face on it too.

When conservatives left the campus to the leftists it was the closing of the American mind sis.

## SAY "NO!" TO PAST THOUGHTS

Toxic past thoughts should be greeted with "NO!" Jesus died to erase the past/come back to NOW.

# FRIENDS WITH BENEFITS

The death of Jesus is sufficient to wipe out your embarrassing past. A Christian knows this best.

## DETOXING FROM MARIUJUANA

They see pot as innocent--but try detoxing from it! You'll be sweating and shaking, hating it.

Cannabinoid hyperemesis syndrome: once pot turns on you to go back is death let alone plain dumb.

CHS is when pot was your friend forever but suddenly became you worst enemy and your killer.

Marijuana: but God didn't make it. They're fiddling so much with strains it's more of a synthetic.

Pot is stored in fat cells. It's like a chicken's skin and when free it goes smooth: outa wrinkle hell.

Old age is not disgrace but they act like it is in ageist cultures. Mass plastic surgeries are no wonder.

Only after detoxing from pot can you TRY to be moderate but by then you won't want it.

It works well at first but now pot is terror, shakes and sweating a lot. I have no desire, thank you God.

## POT DETOX SUX

Pot detox: After going thru all that I'd never go back. Just the thought brings on shakes & sweats.

How different things look free of pot! It was supposed to enhance perception I thought?

Just walking down a country road I have stars in my eyes. I don't need to go anywhere guys.

# FRIENDS WITH BENEFITS

When having a "spiritual experience" on a mind-altering drug, that's a demon-
-but you're a Christian.

Insomnia from pot detox lasted four weeks. Tho' this really sucks now I'm
finally rested and free.

To be sober means just your & God's spirit and nothing else. No demons from
alcohol, pills or pot.

You can be proud of yourself if it's just you in there. Most people use something
else I swear.

If everything you did was being stoned that's why things didn't go right: you
weren't success proned.

Work then relax. You go from the left to the right brain and that's your reward:
not being so taxed.

It's hard when you're off work and wanna smoke, snort or take a shot. Just
relax and that's enough.

# PC MAKES US CRAZY

TYRANNY OF THE GROUP
RECOVERING AFTER BREAKUP
CUT YOUR LOSSES AND GET AWAY
WISDOM TOO HIGH FOR A FOOL
SEX DOES NOT MEAN LOVE
HOW CAN YOU TAKE THIS CRAP?
PERVERTED SEX EXPECTATIONS
EMBRACE PAIN OF WITHDRAWAL
IT'S NOT YOUR SHAME TO CARRY
TOXIC SHAME CURDLING
INNER CRITIC CHANGE BRAIN
ABANDONMENT BRINGS SHAME
COVERT NARCISSISTS ALWAYS BETRAY
THEY ARE WITHOUT CONSCIENCE
I LOVED UNTIL YOU WERE GONE
WORDS PULL YOU DOWN
BE OBNOXIOUS THEN FORGET IT
EVENING THINGS UP:  HOMEOSTASIS
HE STEERS AND DISAPPROVES OF YOU
OLDER WOMEN MUST REMAIN INVULNERABLE
NARCISSISTS CAN'T HAVE RELATIONSHIP
THEY BLOCK OUR SPEECH
WHAT IS A "HATE CRIME"
SUPPRESSION CAUSES EXTREMISM
ARROGANCE OF TYRANNY
DOMESTIC TERRORISTS ARE MOMS & DADS
THE GROSS OPPORTUNISM OF THE LEFT
TRUMP COULD SAVE THE WEST!
CALIFORNIA TERRIBLE/I WAS MISERABLE
DELUSIONAL RINOS IN THEIR SUITS

# PC MAKES US CRAZY

COLLEGES CREATE CRAZED LUNATICS
DISARM VULNERABLE AMERICANS?
SILLY SISTERS LOSE THEIR LUSTER
INVETERATE CLIQUE OF EVIL DOERS
CRAZED AND FANATIC REBELS
TV MAKES SLUTS LOOK CUTE
CONSTANTLY STIRRING THE POT
AMERICA IS TWO PARALLEL UNIVERSES
REVITALIZATION MOVEMENTS IN HISTORY
LOSE FREEDOM, IT DOESN'T COME AGAIN
GUNGRABBERS MAKE US TARGETS OF MAGGOTS
IF IT'S POPULAR THEY GO ALONG WITH IT
CIVIL FORFEITURE: ROBBING YOURS
ARMED SOCIETY IS POLITE SOCIETY
CRIMINALS DON'T FOLLOW LAWS/GET GUNS
AMERICA ON THE RAZOR'S EDGE
DIMINISHED MILITARY AND CONFUSED SOCIETY
ANYTHING GOES BRINGS DEPRESSION YA KNOW
DEMOCRATS THE PARTY OF WAR
TYRANNY BLOCKS PERSONAL PROGRESS
CAMPUS CARRY VS. KILL ZONES
SMART DRESSERS ALWAYS SMILING, BUT...
STRIFE: BECOME FEMINIST TO PLEASE WIFE
NOT OPEN BORDERS BUT "TONE OF VOICE"
FAMOUS FEMINIST IS A LOUSE
RIGHT SIDE OR WRONG SIDE
GANGSTER CULTURE IS CIA-CREATED
OBAMA: 8 YEARS OF TORTURE
BIBLE SAYS: AVOID DEBATE!
BLM IS A FAKE LIBERAL NARRATIVE

# PC MAKES US CRAZY

## TYRANNY OF THE GROUP

Retirement is not being part of the herd anymore--no more expectations or conformity whores.

Retirement is like fame: By now you're behind a locked gate and can do anything you want ok.

In Borrego my life was an open book, they thought me a kook. Now my life is my own and on TOP.

Every little thing they'd criticize. They'd look me up and down and surmise. They'd peg me/all lies.

They loved being the in group who did the judging when they had me over a barrel and struggling.

When it comes time for abuse trials, the flying monkeys are the hit men for their narcissist friend.

People love to be malicious in a group. They compete who is crueler when spreading the scoop.

## RECOVERING AFTER BREAKUP

How does she recover from broken consciousness and emptied self-esteem after a split from he?

It's a traumatic reality she comes to terms with: being used, bamboozled--how to recover from that?

It's not outa weakness that it hurts so bad, it's because of the hope that she had, a mirage: trashed.

She thought this was it. Finally she can end her search and live her life as a partner, completed.

# PC MAKES US CRAZY

But he was in a transactional mode, in it for what he could get out of it. Lovebomb, reject.

It is very heavy to find out someone was just running a game. Heartbreak: emotionally she's insane.

It's the reason she's frantic and sick. She's been playing a losing game, blindsided not weak.

You have to cut your losses not think you must continue since you already have so much invested.

## CUT YOUR LOSSES AND GET AWAY

No matter what your losses you must get away from this table, the game is rigged and he's impossible.

When you realize you're losing you gotta stop playing. He's gone: lost interest/met another/moved on.

Older women must counsel youth just starting: don't fall in love then waste decades: reject him.

"If I lose weight/give him more sex I can make him love me." NOT: it's a rigged system so just stop.

You can't recover from a game while still in the game. You're removed to heal then live again.

Can a sick love addict even see that to stay in a losing situation [over and over again] is insane?

The necessary truth she hates to hear: You are NOT gonna turn this around, no fairy tales here.

It was a nightmare from the beginning but you were so blindsided in love you weren't truly seeing.

The only way is to separate yourself from the source of your poison [pain]. No contact is the only way.

# PC MAKES US CRAZY

No contact is the beginnings of no impact. You lock all the gates coming into you even if you're sad.

## WISDOM TOO HIGH FOR A FOOL

Wisdom is too high for a fool. You want to rise to a much higher dimension above him too.

You isolate for emotional/psychological insulation. See him as poison cuz that's what he is man.

Older women who've been thru this scene had changed attractions from handsome to wholesome.

From cute and trendy to reliability, love consistency, home life that he makes possible for thee.

From a flashy dresser and social climber to a nice guy who pays the bills on time and loves yer.

Give up on this and find a dependable and decent nice man who just wants tranquility/home.

People today don't seek marriage as before, and they game you cuz that's what computers are for.

It's all about sex but starts with lovebombing. We love hearing that, us trauma bonded darlings.

Women want desperately to think sex means love but it doesn't, you're just another dumb broad.

## SEX DOES NOT MEAN LOVE

It'd be great if sex meant love--no problems then. But it doesn't, you've been gamed and scammed.

A trauma-bonded female wants to merge with him as fusion takes place. What about after--same?

# PC MAKES US CRAZY

After sex he says "get your things" and her heart sinks cuz underneath she knows everything.

After their sex session he may not call for days. Then the calls start again, the cycle from hades.

## HOW CAN YOU TAKE THIS CRAP?

Some can take this crap but it's so insincere and using [of something so sacred] she'd rather be dead.

The smart woman has a reliable husband who pays the bills and invests wisely. Not one like your guy.

A smart lady seeks a nice husband who loves home and maintains and protects it, never to roam.

Homelife is so wonderful a man will go to war to protect it: home is country, home is everything see.

Not this gigolo you know, who never follows thru and has no interest in homelife--he's a lowlife.

Not this jerk who just wants sex and drops by whenever then leaves without a thought ever.

Finally, allow no bootie calls--sex favors with exes or drop ins. To a lady this is preposterous sin.

## PERVERTED SEX EXPECTATIONS

All he wants is oral sex: don't give into this. Why adapt to his porn, the whole dam culture's sick.

If you want to, fine. But it's the perverted expectations we're subjected to which you must discern.

"He demanded oral reciprocation and I felt degraded and told him to go to hell"--smart girl.

# PC MAKES US CRAZY

If you want to, fine. It's the sick culture's degraded expectations that youth must discern, aye.

Sex is made as common as going to the bathroom. It's not erotic it's brazen, flat and gross too.

If you want to fine, but expectations are imprisonment and one must be STRONG to go against it.

Politically correct assumes these things are right but spiritually they're a blight--stay home tonight.

You must pull yourself away from him to heal, insulate and then reinforce a transformed mind.

Your mind has been renewed when away from him. You must protect this new growth thru isolation.

You can't be insulated until separated. As the bible says you must "come out from among them."

If soul is insulated a queen conscious woman can go into a sex-sick culture and not be affected.

The problem is most women are released into a toxic world without insulation. Protect em son.

## EMBRACE PAIN OF WITHDRAWAL

It's going to hurt and part of you will long for him--your oppressor abuser, user of a body to ruin.

Embrace the withdrawals you know will hurt, like a addict in pain cuz he knows that comes first.

Know it's gonna hurt as your shift levels from being a Ph.D. fooled by a clown to truly renowned.

Pain is weakness leaving the soul. Moving into a healthier place is the pain we feel that's all.

# PC MAKES US CRAZY

They didn't know anything about her, just assumed she was nuts from what her husband said sir.

The trauma is so embedded in consciousness one is not aware he has shame based problems.

She feels unlovable, unworthy and defective. It's all shame but something she never elected.

Such common traits of toxic shame victims, maybe most of the population in this generation.

## IT'S NOT YOUR SHAME TO CARRY

Shame is internalized after being **DUMPED** from a narcissist onto you as leverage, as they do.

The inadequate older sisters took **THEIR** shame and dumped it onto the empath, just sayin'.

If it's not resolved this shame leads to anxiety, depression, eating disorders, aggression.

It was not my shame or guilt to carry but how'd I know that then, I had feelings of a catastrophe.

Perfect Coo Coo: Extreme perfectionism is rooted in toxic shame and abuse-- who knew?

Unhealthy codependent relationships as adults, all linked to toxic shame introjected first.

Thank your toxic shame abusers for making you into perfectionist world famous mind-cruisers.

World famous beautiful actresses unable to watch their own movies, all from toxic shame probably.

Every culture or tribe has a different roadmap to be ashamed of, a different groove or brainwave.

# PC MAKES US CRAZY

If one's parents were crazy alcoholics then you know their implants were distorted and lunatic.

If one's mother was a crazy liberal feminist then you know her implants were distorted and lunatic.

And these distorted implants are all based on shame since that's the game, it gets you going.

## TOXIC SHAME CURDLING

My shame makes my blood curdle with embarrassment--that's all memory stored beneath the neck.

It goes to the brain to justify the action, not as reason for it--the body response is automatic.

You don't know anything about joker yet you wanna have his children/leave your nice husband.

Just by this education you'll recover completely, despite shame originating in childhood trauma.

The shame stung me with adrenalin with every memory. That's the serpent and education helped me.

Toxic shame is literally enmeshed in cellular memory--IN the brain which is never the same truly.

One was traumatized and thus is having a trauma response to it--shame--and results therein.

## INNER CRITIC CHANGE BRAIN

To heal, engage the inner critic: listen to what you say, what you say to yourself, how you speak it.

We can change our brain. We can affirm that we ARE lovable--taking false memories captive again.

# PC MAKES US CRAZY

If one is experiencing toxic shame it's rooted in abandonment as narc is the attention-hog.

The narcissist wants all the attention on herself not you, so at those times she dumps shame too.

You were abandoned for being yourself so your healing is reconnecting to that true self, do it now.

## ABANDONMENT BRINGS SHAME

Abandonment from the pack brings shame in wolves who die of starvation: a similar situation.

You nurture your inner child--who you know--and come home to yourself. No more shame bashing.

We literally change the brain with positive instructions to it: love, peace, healing, abundance.

It's a beautiful thing to transform your life from the inside out--thinking, speaking then living it.

In abandonment one loses his authentic self and ceases to exist psychotically--very scary.

Healing the shame that binds you: it's internalized when one is abandoned. Know this, heal.

Self-compassion is the most important thing to let go of emotions such as toxic shame and blame.

Self-compassion incinerates the nastiness relatives dumped on you so they could accrue.

Tho' we're imperfect we have wonderful qualities and we focus on those now, not shame honey.

What's loving, what's kind, what brings you peace, the things in your world so sweet: now reap.

# PC MAKES US CRAZY

Focus on uplifting thoughts to change your life, produce magnificence and personal significance.

Victims of toxic shame feel they're never enough, their lives unimportant--so be gentle with self.

We must literally wash ourselves with empathy, compassion & positivity after such treachery.

That humans have the gift to change their brainwaves by what they speak, that's not voodoo see.

Instead of sinking in your swill of bad memories just respeak everything cuz it's all false anyway.

You must have emotional support to end trauma from abusive relationships: God/angels/spouse/pets.

## COVERT NARCISSISTS ALWAYS BETRAY

Covert narcissists always betray you. They do a dirty work under the radar, in secret too.

They fake empathy of your pain but thrive in secret fantasies of raising self up as you're replaced.

Most people are completely fooled by the Clever Covert with impeccable camouflage of a curse.

Coverts talk in self effacing and humble ways about themselves while making sure you hear it all.

They play "just plain folks" while telling themselves how superior they are, not to be unequally yoked.

They play the role of servant while being highly competitive and even meanspirited.

They plot ahead how they will defeat you and they shrewdly understand your weak spots too.

# PC MAKES US CRAZY

Appearing to be a friendly concerned friend or sibling the CC will seduce your spouse darling.

Once she chooses a plan of action she moves forward in force to get exactly what she wants hon'

**THEY ARE WITHOUT CONSCIENCE**

Operating in the psychological shadows the CC has discarded you before you feel the blow.

There are no pangs of conscience only brags of victory. Conscience is not getting caught in reality.

Starlet: The narcissist collects admirers and followers like charms on a solid gold bracelet.

Pseudo-empathy and false humility: the highly polished narcissists have all these things.

Research the condition. You'll hear them praising you, masters of flattery and skilled acting.

Step outa their path and move in your own way. There's many who'll wanna know the real you ok.

We create or destroy with our energy. Sin is the one, repentance is the other and I'm now happy.

The "feminist" colleges encourage women having sex without marriage and now they're powerless.

You keep going after clowns in a crown then slip down, off the frequency where kings speak renowned.

His talk of sex can form a soul tie. Don't allow this, stay real high. Words have power sis, they lie.

From trusting everybody to trusting no-one: this shows you've grown tho' the left will put it down.

# PC MAKES US CRAZY

I grew a shell after being wide-opened. What a fool I was, in maturity I self-forgave for coping mistaken.

## I LOVED UNTIL YOU WERE GONE

Oh! How I loved you, until you were gone. Then I woke up to my own reality and Oh! How it has shone!

I was young and foolish, didn't know what I was doin'. I never knew I was lost til you were gone.

Don't worry, relax. Most are dead and those alive will catch you in new webs cuz God removed the hex.

You only got hurt cuz you didn't know enough to protect yourself. Without a wall or fence evil flows in.

Those backstabbers coming and coming and coming until I had to relocate. The O'Jays 1972

Those backstabbers coming to my house again and again and again and again. The O'Jays 1972

He chose your precious talents but also your proclivities when doing things you shalt not.

Don't worry they're either dead or will catch you in new webs cuz God removed a hex way back.

All kinds of stuff happens when controlled by a demon so see the whole bad era that way and forget it.

## WORDS PULL YOU DOWN

A real man will NEVER use his words to pull a woman down. But most will so stop fishing in the same pond.

They will shame you, belittle and break you down. A queen stays above this by being READY, that's all.

# PC MAKES US CRAZY

Queens know: A man the world rates as a 10 can be a 3, and he who's a 3 may really be a 10, see?

I have enough problems without pulled down by women and some men: awareness is my defense.

There was far more respect for women before feminism. As the weaker sex men didn't degrade em.

When feminism came along it was adversarial and competitive and weak men attacked.

A woman who's a ten and a man who's a 3: he's compelled to bring her down for to even things up, see?

If a man tears her down in any way--just one word--it's water seeking it's own level so stay away.

## BE OBNOXIOUS THEN FORGET IT

To do ridiculous, obnoxious and outlandish things was part of your energy bracket but now it's all legit.

Yes I was crazy/obnoxious/ridiculous but now it's honed down, constrained, I'm all focused on it

A trauma bonded woman follows her abuser to the ends of the earth: know this to gird up/end curse.

When hurtful words bring her back into the ring to avoid his rejecting, that's the insanity/fatality.

The world judges by outer appearances/surface: he's a 3. God judges not by car but heart: he's a 10.

A real man never throws your history back in your face. It's only little boys who fight with women ok?

## EVENING THINGS UP:  HOMEOSTASIS

# PC MAKES US CRAZY

There's a whole lot of men who hate women. They lure submission then go to work down-pulling em.

CRUEL: That's what it is when evening things up in order to maintain their identity of being on top.

Why would you keep reaching out to a man who is breaking you down on purpose friend?

He runs you through with words sharp as knives. As a trauma bond develops you love him more, no jive.

I was insane to ever let him in my home because then I had to put up with him with no protection.

The words can cause irreparable damage to your soul. And yet you stick around cuz your self worth's old.

A single woman should never let a man in her home unless chaperoned. It just doesn't look good doll.

I naively believed everything they would say and got into so much trouble that way. Wisdom: stay away.

And why would you feel SHAME in leaving such a man? Cuz that's the feeling rejected from the pack.

Here you're a TEN and this dude who's a THREE has convinced you he's better than you see.

Women by nature are sensitive to opinions of men, wanting to be led and adapting to something he said.

And so you take his opinions very seriously even making a fool of yourself in your loyalty, that was me.

## HE STEERS AND DISAPPROVES OF YOU

In steering your life as an independent achieving woman, the first thing he does is to disapprove of you.

# PC MAKES US CRAZY

He slides in like Prince Charming and you let your guards down. It's alarming but soon your life is gone.

Especially if she has sex, her heart is open. Now he shoots darts of disapproval and she's broken.

Now she's in the Approval Trap: Living her life for approval of a man who disapproves/always on attack.

Women aren't judging character but what they drive and how they dress: superficial characteristics.

Once lured by a superficial man he begins to erode her soul with hurtful and demeaning words.

Don't allow inferiors to manipulate you. You must stop showing up for it/be clear as a ruling Queen too.

It starts with her as a queen and this means: transcending addictions to relationships/non-ordained sex.

Refusing to partake in non-ordained sex breaks free from soul ties and reverts back to discovery of Self.

By coming back to self you reach a point where you become what you will attract, age irrelevant.

When he said "what you yapping about?" It was a revolution in my head/never saw him again.

## OLDER WOMEN MUST REMAIN INVULNERABLE

In an ageist culture the future is bleak. That's the wrong viewpoint since older you're at your peak.

Especially if a woman is older she cannot allow one word of dishonor or disrespect or it's psychic death.

What an older woman goes thru in society as she ages is outrageous but can be turned into greatness.

# PC MAKES US CRAZY

All on one day she ages out of perception. She is never seen again, a psychic blow of disconfirmation.

One friggin' word and you're out buddy. You have no idea what an older woman suffers in society.

An older woman is too-easy a target since she's already lost confirmation/value in the sexual market.

**GREAT OLDER WOMEN**

A great older woman is ready for abuse and never gets hurt but naiveté makes her vulnerable/cursed.

If a man doesn't treat her like a queen [and needles or dishonors her in any way] he's a creep.

No one needs self-love more than the older woman. Focus on this for your achievements and wisdom.

And have **NOTHING** to do with creeps like that ever again. Never settle for less just cuz you're alone.

The hurtful ageist remarks start around thirty. By fifty you ain't got a chance unless you get real savvy.

Ageism is a chance for weak spirits to vent their cruelty without responsibility as aging babies.

We should have all our constitutional rights back soon after the housecleaning which Daddy's doing.

A wicked heart makes you a public friend and a secret enemy to good people. It's inevitable.

A wicked heart becomes a hypocrite to those who are real, all because pollution defines worldview.

You're a public friend but secret enemy because your heart is not right. It's the Jezebel Spirit, divisive.

# PC MAKES US CRAZY

A wicked heart pollutes the language, saying a buncha stuff you shouldn't as secret sins are revealed.

A wicked heart skews a view of the world. Unto the pure all things are pure but a dirty mind sees weird.

## NARCISSISTS CAN'T HAVE RELATIONSHIP

The narcissist cannot have relationship due to his lack of empathy and pervasive sense of grandiosity.

Contempt, contumacy, superior attitude, self-contained---hmm sounds like me, guess I'm a narcissist.

Culture teaches mental illness and what is seen as mental illness in any era in any place on earth.

Withdrawal, emotional aloofness/flatness, hypo-reactivity, sex without involvement, depersonalization.

We REACT to things like social expectations communicated thru agents and our personality says "I hate it".

The child deals with the bad/dysfunctional mother by internalizing her bad part to not blame her.

The child with the split ego/introjected bad mother archetype can become a sadistic type.

## THEY BLOCK OUR SPEECH

We must attack the tyranny of political correctness blocking our speech-- that is key.

Trump's is a message of common sense cuz we're being led by stupid evil people and pretense.

The Nazis were national socialists. It has never worked but dumbass liberals still insist.

# PC MAKES US CRAZY

Many were held down by liberals in their family. It took em decades of dung to see the true enemy.

Build them up. The feminists put men and marriage as the adversary--the end of you and me.

## WHAT IS A "HATE CRIME"

What's a "hate crime"? Well it all depends who's defining hate doesn't it. Bill Lockwood

The biblical view of marriage they define as hate speech. That's why you're strapped to say anything.

They don't want any opposition--they want an EMPTY playing field. Sandy Mitcham

We're supposed to pay reparations internationally for climate sins--to the biggest polluters.

We're supposed to pay every black person a million something which will bankrupt us hon'.

Have nothing to do with the fruitless deeds of darkness, but rather expose them. Ephesians 5:11

As our rights are taken away China is rising simultaneously--do you see any treachery?

Their knowledge of gov. comes from "Hamilton" and their view of middle Americans "Rosanne" reruns.

He preaches "healing and unity" but that's followed by his friends eradicating all dissent swiftly.

Have NO debate on violence at the capital without including six months of violence from Antifa.

God wants us to be paired up so if you stay alone/work on yourself gravitational pull is the magnet.

# PC MAKES US CRAZY

Worrying and talking about voter integrity is now defined as sedition and soon it may mean prison.

If you're concerned about election integrity you don't deserve free speech/should be impeached.

If you're questioning elections you're inciting violence. Have you heard anything so far-fetched?

George Floyd died and it's all over but who cares about a white female military Trump supporter.

God controls everything: battlefields, families, stars in sky, whales in the ocean, sparrows, all countries.

They're gonna come for us using incitement to violence as the precept and all free speech clipped.

If you say anything other than "I condemn right-wingers" it will be called "incitement to violence" sir.

## SUPPRESSION CAUSES EXTREMISM

Government actions to suppress extremism will inevitably and always cause it. Tucker Carlson

U.S. is trending towards secession for there can be no peaceful coexistence between us and them.

Peaceful coexistence between two completely different theories of life, living and faith in God?

We can't co-exist with some who are constantly deriding, derogating and making us look dumb.

There's no way I can co-exist with a liberal thinking like they do, I'd run from their presence too.

You'd have to be a dumb bum listening to wifey who thinks like that. You're as bad as her, a democrat.

# PC MAKES US CRAZY

Having the election stolen has suddenly brought us together. There's gonna be a backlash sir.

With a week left a petty/vindictive Nancy Pelosi threatens to impeach unless he resigns, see?

Pelosi's answer is to demonize and silence her critics. Or put em in jail--what she likes best.

Always knew you were a dumb bum, an affluent liberal from the coast with nothing goin' on at most.

For you to think these crazy things adapting to your wife makes you so ineffectual, dull and fullabull.

The excited jubilation of the left: they're actually making lists of who's gonna be banned next.

I'm in a safe state [Northern Arizona] away from your hate and fenced in with a wonderful locked gate.

## ARROGANCE OF TYRANNY

There is a tyrannical streak when people are shut up/shut down--you can hear it in their voice man.

The Nazis danced around the fire of book burning. They were jubilant cuz that's what this is honey.

They kicked the hornet's nest, now the divisions are manifest. You'll never hear from me you pests.

Unlike Trump the left doesn't care that you lost your business, just shut the hell up and trust us.

911 was instantly seized upon to institute a whole set of new laws--this will be no different, oh God!

Their gameplan: Inflate the risk of white supremacist terrorism then monitor the hell out of them.

# PC MAKES US CRAZY

Big tech censors enemies of the democrat party who controls key committees to do their bidding.

Big tech giants control everything and we are subject to their undemocratic, unaccountable whims.

It's an initiation of a new war on terror and WE are the terrorists--peace/family-loving Americans.

They will now criminalize "domestic terrorism" by expanding their powers to monitor the same.

## DOMESTIC TERRORISTS ARE MOMS & DADS

The greatest threat to national security is not China or Iran but Innocent Americans: dads and moms.

Media shower: increase fear levels about Donald Trump--it's been the key to their profits and power.

How we treat terrorists: monitor, surveil, DETAIN em. Bully em/allow bullying without consequence.

Draconian state powers being planned/lists being made but Trump's got something else up his sleeve.

They don't want debate, they don't want conversation, they wanna silence you period or be crushed son.

If white America doesn't overcome it's insecurity about being called racist the left will be a success.

If Americans don't get over this inputed white guilt we'll be paying reparations soon cuz they couldn't.

Naive white Americans in principal have guilt over even being associated with this historical evil.

Liberalism is the great oppressor of Black America. Constitutional principals not identity is power.

Our race is our POWER: that was the evil sanctioning slavery/Jim Crow but we see it again now.

Now 75 million Trump supporters are subhuman. They must be punished, restrained, punished again.

# THE GROSS OPPORTUNISM OF THE LEFT

It's the gross racial opportunism of the left. They change their race/divide or blame, whatever it takes.

Condescending partisan elitism: arrogant. Some day soon you won't have your nose in the air like that.

Are they kidding? Fox news asks if the twitter ban was "justified" on our president? Just wait buddy.

They'll come to your door, they'll ram the door down. They'll kill your dog then detain/your gone.

"You must properly store your weapons" rule means they are gonna have to snoop in your house.

They don't want free speech nor freedom at all/won't let you defend it with the 2nd amendment.

## TRUMP COULD SAVE THE WEST!

Trump could save the west! He could save us from disasters like London's Muslim mayor.

Security, borders, one-man-one-vote. That's the free nation that the liberals seek to demote.

Trump is the antidote to Obama (god of gas): He's heaven's escape from the criminal class.

# PC MAKES US CRAZY

Trump has the capability to mold us to a new national sovereignty and it's our heyday.

Coal is the cheapest and cleanest but since the shutdowns we now pay twice as much, no jest!

FI: Feminist Influence, or FI: Feminine Influence. One is bad and the other is good, understood?

As sex becomes mundane, doctors ask voyeuristic questions and there is no more shame.

Giant golden parachute while she's firing people--that's Carly Fiorina, another globalist evil?

Subterfuge was over: the mask ripped off to reveal the phony Obama and criminal takeover.

Our coal could burn for one thousand years and it's completely clean in the scrubbers, Obummer!

They wanna make us dependent and dumb us down. It's all spin cuz they see us as clowns.

Megalomaniacs go all the way when cornered and that's why they've taking it this far.

## CALIFORNIA TERRIBLE/I WAS MISERABLE

California was terrible and I never knew why I was so miserable until I saw it was the liberals.

The more criminals get away with something the more reckless they get and it's their neck.

They're so into the perks they feel infallible and invincible and that blinds the jerks.

Delusions of megalomania: With more power they feel invincible and it's death from schizophrenia.

# PC MAKES US CRAZY

Arrogance won't back off--feeling invincible--and so inevitably loses (inversion principle).

The rep party died long ago but is rising again through Trump--It's the phoenix, destiny, outa the slump.

All media is just priming your mind with predictive programming so you'll accept evil in the future.

As they dig their grave they continue to act as though they're all the rave-- that's the sinner, ok?

The Priebus-Ryan plan to steal what the people want has been exposed (they can't pull it off).

The gender debate is to confuse and sexualize children--perversion even worse then Bill Clinton.

Perversion-training of kids is a way totalitarians bully us--a reality rape, can't you see this?

## DELUSIONAL RINOS IN THEIR SUITS

Paul Ryan is the boy toy of the house. It's a bunch of guys in fancy offices delusional in their suits.

In every slave culture the women have authority over the men--it's an inverted system.

The men are arrested development babies and the wife plays their mom, not a true lady.

Paul Ryan is a sell-out in the right suit: arrogant, frat boy, just a kid, nobody, punk, piece of crap.

The oldest trick in combat is to bluff you're the victor hoping the adversary concedes a loss.

Flip-flop: When suddenly you hate em. The ones you trusted in government, family or friends.

# PC MAKES US CRAZY

Legacy of perversion. Obama's last antic will become his memory: bathroom buffoonery.

Euphemism of the Obama administration: Criminals are called "justice involved individuals".

Bathroom "incidents" will be the beginning of the end of the public school system as we know it.

The psychotic leftist academics are the dumbest yet most destructive of all: they are a total menace.

The devil gets down and dirty in the short time he has left. Count on it: a huge false flag I'll bet.

Too lazy to study they don't know what it means and don't understand what they're giving up it seems.

## COLLEGES CREATE CRAZED LUNATICS

Colleges create the insane, crazed, diabolic demand that no one ever give anyone any offense.

Self-contradictory and hypocritical, they are inveterate facile liars. Get away, go higher.

Lowlife narcissist: Sensitivity to rebuff from those above, hatred and disdain for those beneath.

Spoiled rotten brats: oligarchs. Diabolical narcissists hate helping people and love to ruin/cripple.

The bathroom fallacy: ideologically extreme, scientifically baseless and hateful of democracy.

Take joy. For this is the breaking point we need to swing back to reality: the parental backlash!

Political correctness gets you to turn off you instincts, life force and common sense: cultural suicide.

# PC MAKES US CRAZY

A non-feminist (pro-life) female is rare and that's why the emotionally deprived stare.

We're on this trip together--a rocky road--so just remember you're the prince and they're the toad.

It's getting so discouraging I want to stop posting but because of Jesus I just keep hoping.

Liberals use "justice" to get their way but conservatives first want "freedom" each and every day.

Mao was a mass murderer but the kids love him wearing T-shirts of him, Che Guevara and Hitler.

Clinton legacy: Wall street payback, offshoring and foreign wars--and you want more?

Even pedophilia goes mainstream after gay marriage lowered the bar, releasing evil galore.

The candidate of reckless foreign intervention is the most dangerous: Hillary Clinton.

The Clinton's massive wealth came from auctioning U.S. policies through State Dept. and their Foundation.

**DISARM VULNERABLE AMERICANS?**

Hillary wanted to disarm vulnerable Americans in high-crime neighborhoods, understood?

"Heartless Hillary" is an apt name as the disarmed/vulnerable Americans are killed or maimed.

Guns defeat violent crime a million times a year (look it up) so it's heartless Hillary we must stop.

Guns are the Great Equalizer for women, children and the elderly yet you want heartless Hillary?

# PC MAKES US CRAZY

Hillary wants the worst criminals released--she wants these animals on the streets!

Hillary wants to take our guns just as hardened criminals are released on the streets: Is God pleased?

Anti-gun executive orders is the behavior of a dictator yet you dumb liberals highly rate her?

Evil spirits infect regions--like osmosis as it creeps into the hearts and souls of innocent Americans.

Americans have been wimped until their will to self-defense is lost and their dreams tossed!

Through your censorship you degraded intelligence--then friends and family became a dunce.

Hillary wants to take away our only means of survival: in horribleness there is no rival.

Good bye Barrack. Don't let the door hit you in the ass and on any more democrats we'll pass.

Does just being a woman make her good? Heck no--more often than not it's a heart of wood.

## SILLY SISTERS LOSE THEIR LUSTER

Sister: You put me down then worship a career criminal like Hillary Clinton and even her Mister?

Why is Lynch given to being such a frontwoman for these despicable murders by vermin?

People are sick of the social warrior garbage: "Do what I say or you're a racist" (heartless).

The social warrior children will never get a job in the real world--there's a karma (see God's word).

# PC MAKES US CRAZY

The bathroom issue is simply the Tyranny of the Minority meant to destroy culture and all decency.

Demons come from lack of moral hardline-ness. All you preachers out there should know this.

They got a useless education and now it's weaponized so they can't see how they've been paralyzed.

The social justice warriors are leading us into road warrior and that's a mob and roving terror.

Guns are the equalizer for kids and old ladies. If she wants to destroy that, she's the enemy.

These violent liberals are like maggots on a dead cow: perverted, obscene, filthy and very mean.

San Diegans voted Trump! It was the most liberal but look at this: a complete reversal!

How to conquer a civilization: confuse 'em. Trump is de-confusing and thus we love 'im.

## INVETERATE CLIQUE OF EVIL DOERS

It's an inveterate clique of evil doers and sellouts--who dress and talk nice as culture dies no doubt.

First they come for the poets and cartoonists as they have most power in the body politic.

Guns are the great equalizer for old ladies and children yet you wanna give them to Hillary Clinton?

Conquer by confusing us, saying there's no boys or girls--good grief that's why we're losin' it.

The good leader reminds the people of the difference between freedom and slavery.

# PC MAKES US CRAZY

It's not that he's doing it--he's been doing it--but that he keeps doing it and you accept it.

It's not an indifferent but a supine congress. They're flat on their back allowing this awful mess.

The Creator made two sexes, each beautifully crafted to fit with and meet the needs of the other.

Venezuela-style Politics of Poverty: That's the modern democrats and Hillary Clinton, really!

A real man is ready to manage people, knowing they're all gonna criticize him: the inferiors ravin'.

Kids are social justice warriors and clearly inferior as they mimic evil of which they are followers.

These arrogant kids scare me. There is no respect, no dignity--they are so obscene, really.

They were taught no boundaries, no limits: the unfathomably evil direction of mental midgets.

These arrogant upstarts call you "old" when they fail to find a flaw. There is no respect, avoid the fog.

## CRAZED AND FANATIC REBELS

The rebels don't know how to think, they're crazy and fanatic: lewd dumbasses and they stink.

They lie by minimizing the data: trivializing what is most important or deflecting to trivia.

Forever and always finding moral equivalence between disparate things-- that's you, you finks.

Leftists and affluent liberals are smooth. They often look better too but are often uncouth.

# PC MAKES US CRAZY

Heartless Hillary ruined whole towns for the sake of her ideology and created world tragedies.

Unfathomably evil direction of mental midgets: that's what we're up against-- need Trump for fences.

100 million killed pursuant to socialism. Yet liberals still want it, ignoring any and all criticism.

Groupthink is being a yes-man.

What is the herd? Through social hypnotism they all agree--It's also called the bell-shaped curve.

What kills the skunk is the publicity it gives itself. Abraham Lincoln

It's their ideology that makes them mentally ill. They act insane from a false premise, that's all.

You misinterpret my Christian restraint as weakness well now I'm gonna come back at your creepiness.

This is a battle between trendiness (empty mindlessness) of fools and those trying to regain true ideals.

Through social hypnotism and the acculturation process an entire culture can fall into evil and possessed.

## TV MAKES SLUTS LOOK CUTE

The Golden Girls made slutsville look cute. To a culture that was the meanest thing to do.

Females have different needs so don't tell me we should act like men sexually--not our destiny.

The only thing that "evens things out" is chastity--or the more emotional female is left or hurt, surely.
The price of liberty is eternal vigilance. From the founders to the wild west, that was the essence.

# PC MAKES US CRAZY

Teach your children to be neat and orderly. Not a bunch of junkards living in chaos and so unmannerly.

Donald Trump is the only thing standing between Christians and death camps. Franklin Graham.

The kids had an edge cuz they were liberal and loud. We caved in but now see them, the devil's crowd.

The problem is not just addiction (habits) but bad associations and their rackets lowering your status.

Like fish, people absorb the filthy waters they swim in. Through social hypnotism/osmosis they sin.

Americana is excellence and perfection. Been a long time but we're back after a national savior won the election.

The whole problem with liberals is they think people are good--except liberty-lovers, the misunderstood.

When a nation comes together to help a city recover it's not the same as a "community organizer".

## CONSTANTLY STIRRING THE POT

Constantly stirring the pot/lighting fires. Saul Alinsky stuff: create the problem then take over.

He acts like we're at each other's throats. We haven't done a thing but its gun control he promotes.

Extremism in the defense of liberty is no vice and moderation in the pursuit of justice is no virtue. Goldwater

Stop trying to explain the details of misbehavior and simply see it as a demon which wins great favor.

Trump's never offended me one bit. What does offend me is the fake niceties of the hypocrites.

# PC MAKES US CRAZY

This man has promoted wickedness: race riots, bathroom perversions and gross crookedness.

Trump doesn't offend one bit it's just the democrat moochers who seek to make him look illigit.

Fanning the flames higher and higher by putting a bee in their bonnet and it was all by Obama.

Status Quo, you know, is Latin for the mess we're in. Ronald Reagan

Though they throw gays off buildings/stone women for being raped, the left aligns with Islam, you say?

Ignore their false promises and rhetoric and look at their track record alone, idiot.

We hated the devil at the helm. All he did was obstruct, frustrate or destroy and we were overwhelmed.

The grossest dictators wear a smile. That's how they turn the knife killing all the while.

Tyrants always get delusional when the people say no, and try to double down to pull us below.

## AMERICA IS TWO PARALLEL UNIVERSES

Americans are dividing between those awake and total dumbed down idiots, perverts and flakes.

The "enemy of my enemy is my friend" is the bottom line of the left's love of unholy swine.

President Obama is the greatest hoax ever perpetrated on the American people. Clint Eastwood

As white people, it's our fault that a black power political group slaughtered cops, that's the scoop.

# PC MAKES US CRAZY

A nation comes together and helps cities recover but when a leader incite riots, a great danger.

I love America because of it's principals and the good works done by prior, more devout generations.

There's no need for you liberal losers to be irate. Why not just embrace what made us great?

When there's no more decency, when no lines are drawn: life is a tragedy and all honor is gone.

When revolution (of minds) begins things solve very rapidly, after long periods with out remedy.

When moral revolution takes off it's like a rocket as true genius is released out of jail or the closet.

Academia is one big leftist gang. They hate conservatives and target them/don't ask them to hang.

When moral revolution takes off it's like a rocket as true genius is released out of jail or the closet.

## REVITALIZATION MOVEMENTS IN HISTORY

Revitalization Movements in history show things can turn around suddenly (through Trump our honey).

He's the only breath of fresh air, only hope we have and sole reason for optimism--or hell with Hill.

Liberal Logic: Cheap, petty, boring, dumbed, idolatrous, shallow, demagogic--and results are tragic.

It's easy for the devil to overcome those who've been taught tolerance, and everyone's a dunce.

The modern church is no longer a comfort with wonders as it shuns doctrine to increase numbers.

# PC MAKES US CRAZY

Instead of dealing with reality they spoke in cheap petty terms dignified by a convention. Donald Trump

DNC: The grandest effort in history to put lipstick on a pig.

Parasites calling modern slavery the "people's system". That's the democrats and it's sick, friends.

Selling favors that sold us down the river. That's Hillary Clinton but even so many still loved her.

Fiction, fraud and fantasy: Satan's proud of Obama's speech and we're still putting up with the leech.

We can't have four more years of abandoning allies and strengthening enemies. Mike Pence

Disattend from liberal idiots quickly now. They may sound convincing but dumb as Rachel Maddow.

Justice warriors (dumbness is rife): There are more important things than your feelings, like your life.

Liberals eliminate things in western society that make it nice to women, gays, blacks, pets--really?

## LOSE FREEDOM, IT DOESN'T COME AGAIN

Those who have known freedom and then lost it have never known it again. Ronald Reagan

Trump is always such a breath of fresh air, and great relief after listening to thieves and liars

Hollywood flesh and hero worship is so embarrassing and boring. Can't they see we're warring?

Unbelievable hypocrisy of low info liberals dumbed down for decades in common core schools

# PC MAKES US CRAZY

Middle aged frumpy Snoop Dog tries to escape irrelevance by releasing ridiculous anti-Trump clown video.

Around-the-clock propaganda against Trump. The wicked and unwise love it and they fear a slump.

Disattend now from all this empty trash. You've gone along with things long enough, a clash.

It's not just about Trump! It's about liberal ascendency for fifty years and how they screwed us up!

I'm not a republican, I'm not a democrat. I'm an American and I want my country back! Sarah Palin

Totally vacuous college girls wanting to live totally promiscuous lives can totally relate to Hillary/lies.

Freedom means free speech not politically correct safe spaces. Ted Cruz

Liberals wanna kill babies and they are perverts. We must face this fact about em though it hurts.

I want the news not boobs. Fox news and even Alex Jones is guilty of using sex to sell to fools.

## GUNGRABBERS MAKE US TARGETS OF MAGGOTS

You've taken away the right of people to defend themselves so now they're soft targets of maggots.

Our main problem is low-information voters. Mainstream news like CNN and MSNBC are lie-promoters

Did your friends/family enable one of the worst criminal takeovers (of our great America) in history?

Weakness arouses evil. That's all we've gotten from the left's "leading from behind": think, people!

# PC MAKES US CRAZY

He's gonna do "dissident extractions" first--take you away. If no Trump, darkness takes over, ok?

The deal's been made to kill the west/shut down true liberalism and is orchestrated by liberals (social fascists).

True feminism: a woman defends herself. State-run feminism: weak, chip-on-her-shoulder, daft.

The west is dying before our eyes due to corrupt, weak, liberal leadership. Michael Savage

We've all been touched by this psychically, if not personally. We all see the darkness of this reality.

He called out Newt for what he said rather than the perpetrators of the tragedy killing 83 dead.

They create the environment that creates the conflict and then they escalate it--hard to believe it?

An assault on law enforcement and open season on decency: the bikers are addressing the tragedy.

## IF IT'S POPULAR THEY GO ALONG WITH IT

Now that it's popular they'll go along with it. They are leafs in the wind--soulless--and I'm sick of it.

What about all the babies killed by these creeps? They'll never be clean again (unless repent, please!)

It's not just about criminal Hillary but all your friends who went along with her--to the pillory.

A win over Obama/Hillary with a Trump ascendency is a settling of all old doubts/scores and more!

God thinks he's an arrogant creep too! He will take care of this as the Vindicator (don't be blue).

# PC MAKES US CRAZY

He perfectly exemplifies the arrogance of liberals. So beyond the pale of entitlement, and soulless.

Police brutality is color-blind: more whites are killed than blacks. See the whole, know the facts.

Haven't we had enough of these fakes, frauds, phonies and backsliders? Be rid of these posers!

A double minded man is unstable in all his ways. He's a liar and thief but bcuz we let him, crime pays.

Martial Law beginnings are called "war games" and that's why they're on the streets, they claim.

What do we want? State's rights. The more local the less devil so just that increases our heights.

Black Liars Murder (BLM) is the result of Pres. stirring the pot then appointing himself to mop it up.

Cops make 12 billion a year taking your stuff/money. Policing for profit's a huge industry honey.

## CIVIL FORFEITURE:  ROBBING YOURS

Civil forfeiture happens in all states. Eating our substance/taking our stuff puts us in dire straights.

Obama pretended--responding to the situation he created to provide pretext for takeover he wanted.

Melanis outclassed Michelle Obama and thus the media's gone insane (at the people's chosen reign).

We have a right to feel safe! But they've made that impossible--as evil exists (but with Jesus we are saved).

The republican platform sought to block slavery and Lincoln was the rep defeating it with the military.

# PC MAKES US CRAZY

Polymorphy is: blurred lines, having many mates. It's a sign of the end times: indecency and hell's gates

The cost of Hillary's dishonesty could be the loss of America as we know it. Newt Gingrich

When Trump gets in we'll be rid of the divisive liberal media: censors, critics and cynics.

The media/politicians will do and say anything to keep their rigged system in place. Donald Trump

Potential vanishes into nothing without effort. Donald Trump

What we went through for 8 years (and 30 before that with family and friends) was from liberal trends.

Donors/lobbyists line up behind Hillary to keep the gravy train rolling and never stop robbing.

Now is the time to ignore everything they say. We've got our man and know he'll save the day.

Never surrender your rights (guns) because once they're gone you'll never get em back (fact).

**ARMED SOCIETY IS POLITE SOCIETY**

An armed society is a polite society. Especially if concealed, one never knows so he acts nicely.

Now's the time to just listen to Trump and ignore his detractors. Not wasting time/hurt is what matters.

The same creepy kids needing "safe zones" are wearing Che Guavira shirts-- what hypocritical jerks.

This business of not letting millions trickle down to those in need is common with the Clintons.

# PC MAKES US CRAZY

You can get a Ph.D. in Global Warming though it's all bull and a hoax. Degrees mean nothing now folks.

The liberals have had control of how we think for fifty years and we're sick of it/reversing out of it.

The crazy liberals are arrogant creeps. These are brats who need to have their face slapped I think.

Democrats: Corrupt from the beginning always under the banner of goodness and right (yet a blight).

The Democrats were corrupt from the beginning since they were for slavery, the KKK and other sinning.

The globalist plan through the democrats: make us poor, stupid and controllable (progressive doormats).

Slave owners and the KKK were democrats and Hillary loves them, that hypocritical dem!

Democrats were slaveowners and the KKK--then they switched it: reps were racists, they were ok.

Hillary Clinton is a risk Americans can't afford to take. Don Trump Jr.

## CRIMINALS DON'T FOLLOW LAWS/GET GUNS

Criminals by definition don't follow laws. Don Trump Jr.

See Hillary's America! Democrats were the meanest slaveowners ever--they are criminals!

With the Clintons, nothing is sacred and everything's for sale. Donald Trump

Anyone calling Trump a "racist sexist homophobe" is just parroting the globalist-owned news folks.

The way you've gone along with this horrible dark thing, thinking it's "IN" makes you crap and me king.

# PC MAKES US CRAZY

The Democrats formally nominated the most scandal-plagued and disliked candidate in their history.

For years the more dirt they got on others the less dirt--though exposed-- stuck to them but no more I wager.

Just because you're black doesn't mean you have to vote democrat. Diamond and Silk

Hill-pocrisy: True to form, her speech was riddled with mistruths, equivocations and lies.

The devil's not a maker--the less they give, they're a taker. Its so sickening with the plot thickening.

We've reached the point of total disrespect and cutting all ties to liberals and their endless lies.

Liberals dress in white to appear pure. They detest the one who wears the dark, though a seer.

We're concerned that this is not a good thing but will it not trigger revolution- -a swing?

Why did this miscarriage of justice happen? Because they all have dirt or they plant it on em.

## AMERICA ON THE RAZOR'S EDGE

America will either be hammered or Trump will nail it. There is no lukewarm but God can help it.

Please God revive the American spirit. We've been overcome with evil and our dark future, I fear it.

The constitution is a beautiful document. It is so efficient you can fit it in your pocket. Paul Ryan

"Get the treatment they need" means incarceration in a cold heartless camp and never freed.

# PC MAKES US CRAZY

"Mental health system" may mean a database of those who won't conform to evil or be debased.

Friends and family must be confronted: did they enable this criminal takeover by how they voted?

Any nation calling good evil/evil good is mad. The contagion of madness shows across the land.

Please God let goodness prevail. These criminals are dark forces and perverted as hell!

At first, patriotism brings scorn. But later, when it costs nothing, they all jump on, like a swarm.

How long before it's old news? Get your life back: think eternally not temporally (blues).

Bottom line of left's love of swine: your enemy makes me love you cuz they're no friend of mine.

## DIMINISHED MILITARY AND CONFUSED SOCIETY

Diminished military, confused society, coarsened culture or Trump: renaissance or slump?

Don't get discouraged, the creeps are still in power so course they'll ratchet it up to the last hour.

Cause riots to give cops the best tools to cope, then federalize it all: it's all about control.

Two powers in the world: sword and mind. In the end the sword is always beaten by the mind. Napoleon

Liberals always blame others for what they do. Don't get caught up in their guilt projections (dudu).

The left "protects Muslims" by embracing Wahhabism's most sexist standards.

# PC MAKES US CRAZY

The Canadian is sick but because he looks slick (like Obama) the dumb voters are thick as bricks.

For Obama if there are blacks in prison, its racism. He doesn't consider other factors, ma'am.

One thousand people die a month from TB and our gov does nothing cuz destroying the country is it's thing.

Did the snake trigger the shootings? Yes of course and everyone knows that's why we're losing.

The pea brains who can't think for themselves get it from their music, agitators and other traitors.

Civil war has begun but the police will ban together so as not to be killed one by one and it won't be fun.

We're so sick of the Clintons. The chicaneries and outright robbery by them and all their minions.

## ANYTHING GOES BRINGS DEPRESSION YA KNOW

Your depression began when told "anything goes". Joy comes from restraint (from one who knows).

Imminent change: a false flag by democrats losing power/gravy train, or Nibiru--one and the same?

Obama's more "presidential" than Trump--no matter that he ruined America/put us in a sad slump.

As soon as the false flag/Nibiru occurs, he'll come for the guns: gangs invade and nowhere to run.

Trump doesn't offend one bit it's just the democrat moochers who seek to make him look illigit.

The Khans are the latest grieving victims the Dems use to attack as media obsesses one-tracked.

# PC MAKES US CRAZY

There's been a turnaround, revolution has begun. The hypocrites lost and the people's desires won.

The enemedia went into "full Soviet" last week. It's part of the criminal machine and denial is bleak.

We will remember later, you awful collaborators--ganging up on the best country's only savior.

When you can't make a dent just retreat til' apathy's spent then return as a good lady or gent.

Donald: don't let their disapproval restrain your speech one bit--ignore them/be yourself: legit!

A rigged system and dishonest media. That's what we're running against: boldface lies or trivia.

To run this country we need a badass with sass. Not these wimps so morally lowdown too (no class).

## DEMOCRATS THE PARTY OF WAR

Democrats are the party of war. Not the republicans--they end wars but are called hawks more.

Obama: Trump's unfit--"doesn't know economics or the constitution"--but look in the mirror you twit.

Trump's making his list of liars and collaborators:  the entire old guard and RINO fakers.

Trump's handsomer each speech cuz the animating contest of liberty brings out one's best.

Which "F.I." is your home--Feminist Influence (bad) or feminine Influence (makes everyone glad).

We don't have a problem with the constitution just lawless politicians like Hillary Clinton.

# PC MAKES US CRAZY

President Obama will go down as the worst president in the history of the United States. Donald Trump

Common core is so filthy. How dare you do that to our kiddies--you perverts are shameless and guilty.

Save us father, let Donald begin.  In Jesus' mighty name, amen.

You better hope you die or Trump wins. Your whole world will degrade to poverty=nothins'

Eliz. Warren: cute little jackets with Neru collar and 3/4 sleeves won't keep you warm on the streets.

Hillary Clinton would be horrifyingly corrupt as president and a disaster in foreign policy again.

This is our chance to overthrow special interests and restore rule by the people after so much evil!

## TYRANNY BLOCKS PERSONAL PROGRESS

It's about self-discovery, expansion and enlightenment (genius) vs. tyranny (censured and joyless).

Even if Trump died the movement would go on, for the new lines of revolution have been drawn.

They're all about building their empires not protecting our lives. That's why no empathy, and lies.

Keep the problem going so the money keeps flowing. Even though lives are lost they act unknowing.

Millenials blame America for the fix we're in. They don't realize it was the democrats (a trash bin).

The real moral burden lies with those refusing to oppose the frightening candidacy of Hillary Clinton.

# PC MAKES US CRAZY

Pray to God for our country (pray for Trump). Pray that right prevails and we'll get over the hump.

Booze: fun when it's goin' down but a little later or in the morning life is trashed/you're in mourning.

It was the Golden Girls who debased women into debauchery. For godly ladies it is filth and mockery.

Not true: "men were mean to women in the past". They respected/protected cuz both had class.

Older women go for younger men but have to educate the puppy. It's not a feather in your cap lady.

If the central government becomes destructive of our rights, the second amendment ends the fight.

Henry the VIII Syndrome: Wanting to get rid of wife he accuses her of adultery to ruin/end her life.

## CAMPUS CARRY VS. KILL ZONES

Campus carry eliminates kill zones in school. The students can finally rest easy and just be cool.

It's not him it's who he delegates to get jobs done and we have faith he'll choose rightly, each one.

Of course he was trying to destroy this country. There should be no question about this tragedy.

Forget unity: Jesus never came to unite but to divide us from significant others/people who bother.

Trump's the real deal and thus they're throwing everything they've got against him. Alex Jones

The country started when they came to get the guns: added the 2nd amendment, then we won.

# PC MAKES US CRAZY

Most men aren't leaders, they follow the women. Women make the decisions though lacking vision.

Voting for Trump was the Christian thing to do. For Hillary is a criminal/would've crushed America and soon.

The sands of time that made this country great are running low. Alex Jones

It's a limited democracy--51% can't consign the 49% to slavery cuz it's constrained by law, see?

Charity for some should not compromise security for all. Governor Gregg Abbot

The insanity of liberalism: thinking "everybody's good". They don't see them as evil just "misunderstood".

We lost the 4th estate years ago. Now it's run by monstrous left-wing fanatics hating America as foe.

They hate him cuz he's rich and white. This is a terrible situation since in every way he's right.

## SMART DRESSERS ALWAYS SMILING, BUT...

They dress nice always with a smile on their face but see past that cuz in a moment they're disgraced.

If God can save us from this it'll be the biggest miracle in history--that's how bad it is, see?

Liberals do nothing about criminals but yell about guns. They are anti-police and all for the thugs.

Democrats destroyed inner cities and drove out jobs, after ruining the schools and tolerating thug fools.

We have a tinker toy power grid that goes out with inclement weather but about this no one's bitter.

We incarcerate more people than China, a tyranny with 4x the population.

# PC MAKES US CRAZY

Feminism was never about equal pay but destroying the family. Look higher at the evil purpose honey.

Liberals are wicked and crazy. They wanna let violent criminals go free but kill an innocent baby.

Antifa beat up people praying for peace for both sides. Someone's gonna get killed if unreconciled.

Neat: Due to the structure of revitalization movements it'll now be a mass re-adjustment to a new beat.

You can't act that way/do those things and expect God's blessing (that's the old style of preaching).

Both sides are corrupt but we've got an outsider so both sides hate him, got it?

Both sides hate him and via fake media they've a waged a war of LIES and people bought it/despise.

To please his wife he became a feminist but in truth a sadist cuz that's how it works, it's the gist.

## STRIFE:  BECOME FEMINIST TO PLEASE WIFE

For a man to be feminist means he has to gulp so much untruth he's gonna finally erupt/get cruel.

Wouldn't want men to swing to the other extreme like Taliban but they've been wimped by feminism.

Men take the views of their dumbed down wives who've been brainwashed about how to view life.

Men want to please their wives, peace at any price. So they agree with this crap and lose their minds.

And they get vituperative too, having lost the ability to think. Razor sharp minds, steel traps of rinkydink.

# PC MAKES US CRAZY

Rather than studying things deeply they scream insults but it's all so self-discrediting it's funny sort of.

The most popular are meaningless. The social world is clueless and boring to seekers of reasonableness.

Common Core kid books are like pornography. This is trash but we're told it's better than geography.

Liberals will do anything to do conservatives in. They'll defame, wreck and trash their reputation.

This mental revolution is so striking as people collect their thoughts after all the lies they bought.

Cannibus is medical, man. It cures all diseases and keeps us staying happy and thin our whole life span.

Do not concur with youth/immorality just to maintain relationship for that's giving up self/being unfit.

We can't see how bad things really are due to sensory overload and infinite distractions but oh Lord!

**NOT OPEN BORDERS BUT "TONE OF VOICE"**

Liberals aren't talking about open borders, crime, poverty or threats of ISIS just Trump's tone of voice.

Our leaders call our devolution into moral madness "progressivism" but it's sexual perversion/paganism.

He gives a weak speech quickly and gets paid to then change a critical element of foreign policy.

Dumb liberals actually see Sharia as progressive--unbelievably dangerous how they love repressives.

The pressure is building against Barrack Obama and Hillary Clinton across this great and glorious nation!

# PC MAKES US CRAZY

Stop trying to appease people because they are ultimately unappeasable and that means trouble.

It's not just Clintons but the coordination with corrupt media but Trump can undo this in the meanwhile.

I don't put America down we just have to admit we're captured by criminals before turning it around.

With riots comes Martial Law and crackdown. They're foreign bought but some are homegrown.

Clinton Foundation principal: You accuse your opponent of doing what you're doing, always.

As political gangsterism is normalized in America we see massive Stockholm Syndrome and trauma.

Since the sixties it's fashionable to hate America. Through this strategy liberal fools are globalist tools.

If you weren't voting for Trump were you voting for Hillary? Cuz if he lost we'd have gone right into tyranny.

They must blanket us with nonsense because it's so obviously false and so we won't see their faults.

## FAMOUS FEMINIST IS A LOUSE

A famous feminist encouraged her fans to swear and not keep house. Now she's rich, the louse!

Grafters were running for president and no one seemed to care, no wonder we're no longer rare.

Liberals think: Immigrants are the victim. Trumpists think: The victim is the American citizen.

They saw him as creepy, childish, stupid and weak--a limp handshake, demonic, up a creek.

# PC MAKES US CRAZY

He spent all the money on useless wars and refugees then the infrastructure dissolved by degrees.

Increasingly I relate only to Trumpists. The others are working towards our destruction with fascists.

There is a natural division of labor, don't tell me there isn't. Men work the heavy and women light and steady.

How do you grab victory from the jaws of defeat? God does it because it's His battle--how neat!

Cutting taxes is the return of the "big engine". It's prosperity from competition and that is capitalism.

Progressives suggest we should completely abandon Western values to be PC: more liberal insanity.

Regression into ancient pagan sexuality (Sodom Gomorrah type) they call "good" but ya think we should?

Quit seeking/pumping up your likes. Don't you know the most popular are usually meaningless sites?

And that's all she wrote. I'm sick of the news, will just sit back and pray that all goes well for Trump.

## RIGHT SIDE OR WRONG SIDE

If they're not on the right side they're on the wrong--that's evil and the demon possessed, hypnotized throng.

Until they're on the right side they're on the wrong--a canyon between us--so put on a new song.

I didn't like your thing on sex. That was way over the mark, a verbal assault and embarrassing too, a hex.

Shut up about it, get some class. You're socially hypnotized to accept this crap--it's gross and crass.

# PC MAKES US CRAZY

Most people want to look good and they know they don't but don't know why: It's the food.

Women who've been sexually assaulted may become promiscuous believing they're not good enough.

It is easier to fool someone than to convince them they have been fooled. Mark Twain

People don't want to hear the truth because they don't want their illusions destroyed. Nietzsche

Instead of facebook here, I'm happier in prayer. But I always return in fascination to the world's snare.

Give em lip and you're going to jail. People are truckling in fear of government: a fly to a whale.

We're waging the war on corruption by crashing through lies and disinformation. Alex Jones

After eating starch I feel like I ate a couch. It's not my thing but a few nuts seems ok (no ouch).

Fox confirms the left by questioning known liars because they control reality as history's actors.

## GANGSTER CULTURE IS CIA-CREATED

Gangster culture was CIA-created to prep people for prison populations and inciting divisions.

1964 CIA memo: When they won't tow the line we'll call em a "conspiracy theorist" to undermine.

Cause of violence: Media is told to condone thugism so even country music shows destruction.

I too was victimized by the liberal agenda. It takes years to sort it out after mind messes up in America.

# PC MAKES US CRAZY

Start the equality thing and it never stops--like the French Revolution more heads are lopped.

Be "good to all" and never making distinctions between right and wrong--false equivalence is our fall.

We have an easy job: just tell the truth. We don't have to tax our memories by lying/faking like you.

Cries of "racism" is the oldest trick in the Democrat book. We're getting sick of these (Hillary) crooks.

Hitlerian harridans are crueler than men. It's cuz it's not their true nature to mimic to that end.

To cover his tracks with Monica Lewinsky, Bill Clinton bombed Iraq. How epic, worse than Barrack.

Politicos, media hacks, broken borders, bloated bureaucracy, gov that doesn't work and high tax.

They think if they chum up with evil it won't come after them but they'll be the first damned people.

**OBAMA:  8 YEARS OF TORTURE**

8 years of torture from this man--and you're even considering the same thing through Hillary Clinton?

It's beginning to topple then it'll all fall down. That's the way revolution works when full blown.

A lie told often enough becomes the truth. Vladimir Lenin
I don't think of you as a person of "color" but a person, period. But you divide us and it's weird.

They are too dumb to be scared. The low-information voters are naive, dangerous and unprepared.
We'll really see heresy from here on out. The most ridiculous excuses for sermons, no doubt.

# PC MAKES US CRAZY

To blacks: Two times we elected the first black president ever and did your condition get any better?

The B.S. we've been taught: I used to hate it too but It was a set up for destruction--to USA bid adieu.

Bullshit race-baiting leftist narratives is all he's spouting. He's a total fool but they're encouraging.

You can't ignore it til it comes on your doorstep. It's happening we're falling but Trump gives us pep.

Anti-flag stuff started in the sixties with  the creepy hippies so retrieve happies by returning to the fifties.

It was a national curse when the hippies became sexually perverse and the wages of sin is the hearse.

When liberals say to conservatives "you should mature" it means you should "sell out", for sure.

If you wanna learn about Civics, fine. But if you just wanna argue, shut up you're no friend of mine.

**BIBLE SAYS:  AVOID DEBATE!**

I'm not wasting any more energy arguing with you, low brain! You're dumbed down, a ball and chain.

I've allowed you to eclipse my identity by giving you time in my head but no more for you are the enemy.

We need to take action, the gloves are off. We know who you are and we'll stop you, though you scoff.

No matter what you say you're a "racist", "hater", "bigot" and "homophobe". I tell you this is getting old.

Everything is racist and I mean everything. If their song you don't sing you're a worm/they're the king.

# PC MAKES US CRAZY

We'll get the jobs back and have school choice. We'll have renewed prosperity and get back our voice.

None of this is reported on the news, all globalist-owned and run. Even FOX has Saudis on the board, hon'.

To blacks: Two times we elected the first black president ever and did your condition get any better?

Why aren't feminists against Islam? Simple: Either they're chicken or don't know what they're sayin'.

More whites are killed by police and black killings are by other blacks but you won't hear those facts.

## BLM IS A FAKE LIBERAL NARRATIVE

Black Lives Matter is a fake liberal narrative. Only if you go along do you have your first amendment.

If my free speech doesn't go along with them suddenly it's called "hateful" and "divisive" what I said.

B.S. race-baiting leftist narratives is all he's spouting. He's a total fool but they're encouraging.

They don't even know what they're protesting about. No history, no poli sci, no civics--an embarrassment.

Feminist sisters will hold you down. They don't want you doing your thing and will destroy your crown.

Couldn't care less what you liberals think. You stink so please leave, low-thinkers are rinkydink.

The evil rich have hired whole armies against us. Only Trump can solve if we have any chance.

Christianity, conservatism and Trump support is "intolerant, hateful and racist" on campuses nationwide.

# PC MAKES US CRAZY

Trump hates the corruption but not the principals: those "principals for which we stand."

You loved that man, you got him in. You enabled this criminal takeover cuz he justified your sins.

He'll call off the dogs--the spies. He can do that for power trickles down-- what he says goes/spy dies.

The progressives are so insensitive they can't empathize with the victims of ideological directives.

The left was all down on Trump for Russian collusion which was unproven but now they love Putin?

Turn it all off and just listen to Trump. He's our only hope, raised by God to get us over the hump.

# 100 KAREN KELLOCK BOOKS

AFFINITY OR MISERY
AGELESS CORNUCOPIA
AMERICA AWAKE!
AMERICA'S DAFT ERA
ARTS OF PALEO FASTING
AUTOPHAGY ON CHEATERS
BACKSTABBING NEUROTICS
BETRAYAL TRAUMA
BOOMERS AND BROKENNESS
BOOT ON NECK
CHAMPION GUIDES
COMMIE NUTHOUSE
COMMIES
COMMUNIST SPIRIT
CONTAGION OF MADNESS
CONTAGIOUS MADNESS
CULTURE CLASH BASHED
DAFT LEFT
DAILY FASTARIAN
DAM RATS
DIVERSITY IS CRUELTY
E-RACE WHITE
EVIL FREAKS (Beyond Gross)
THE END OR A BEND?
FEMALE BULLIES AND FEMI-NAZIS
FEMALE CARNALITY
FEMALE DUMB DOWN
FEMALE POWER DRIVE
FEMINISM AND RUIN 1 & 2
FIX FOR MISFITS
FOOLS & TRAMPS
FREEDOM SPEAKING
FRENEMY ENABLER
FRENEMY LIAR
FRENEMY THIEF
FRENEMY TRAITOR
TRENEMY TYRANT
GENIUS IS HELD DOWN
GLOBALISLAM
GOD USES THE FLAWED
HAZE OF THE LATTER DAYS

# KAREN KELLOCK PH.D.

M.S. Political Science, San Diego State.  Ph.D. in Psychology, University of California Irvine.  Postdoctoral:  UCI School of Medicine, Dept. of Psychiatry [NIMH Grants].  Developed the Debris Theory of Disease, a theory of system pathology in 120 books and 22 textbooks for the general public.  The theory has a general formula:  All disease is obstruction, all recovery is elimination, all success is attraction.  The three obstructions are people, habit and food. Remove obstruction and snap to your goals, waiting in the wings.

www.ingramcontent.com/pod-product-compliance
Lightning Source LLC
Chambersburg PA
CBHW061728250726
48657CB00002B/823